THE ANIMAL CONNECTION

═══ Share Their True Adventures ═══

HEATHER BROOKS

Copyright © 2018 Heather Brooks
All rights reserved
First Edition

PAGE PUBLISHING, INC.
New York, NY

First originally published by Page Publishing, Inc. 2018

ISBN 978-1-64138-059-1 (Paperback)
ISBN 978-1-64138-060-7 (Digital)

Printed in the United States of America

Foreword

The true animal adventures that emerge from the following stories reflect on each of us. They can compel, as they did me, to become involved with how each animal behaves in its individual situation. Their behavior tells us something about who they are in relation to their surrounding environment and how we impact that environment. The two wolves in "A Tale of Two Wolves" come from opposite environments—one living in a restricted rehabilitation center, the other free to roam within nature's habitat. The "helping hands" that reach out to them add meaning to their lives and ours.

These "helping hands" form an intricate connection to the wildlife around us, from the Los Angeles Zoo to the California Wolf Center. They matter immensely in shaping the direction of wildlife and are invaluable in the services they provide. The added dimension of protection and care these agencies create is what we all want for our animals.

As you read these stories, you may even realize that their yearnings, in a small way, have become yours and may help you to better understand their needs, their interaction with nature, and that they are appreciated. It's a two-way street where humans and animals cross paths and learn from one another along the way.

Let's begin!

Acknowledgments

I am indebted to the following professionals and their agencies for the valuable time and consideration they provided. This book would not be complete without them. Thank you!

Erica Varela, *Los Angeles Times*, Rights and Permission

Christina Souto, associate director of Development and Communication, California Wolf Center

Julianne E. Steers, photographer and marine biologist

Carly Padella, community outreach educator, Project Wildlife

Travis L. Truelove, photographer, North Carolina

Elizabeth Materna, public affairs specialist, US Fish and Wildlife Service, Oregon

John Stephenson, biologist, US Fish and Wildlife Service, Oregon

Cynthia Singleton-Nichols, executive assistant, AeroVironment Inc.

LTJG Chloe Morgan, public affairs officer, Naval History and Heritage Command

Karen Martin, PhD, biologist

Cast of Characters

Reggie The Renegade Alligator

Dolphins Lead The Way

The Surfing Fish

The Case of the Stowaway Albatross

A Tale of Two Wolves

Outfoxing Extinction

Project Wildlife

The Little Flying Machine

Reggie the "Renegade Alligator"

Reggie is in a predicament! Just as he was starting to enjoy his newfound freedom in Los Angeles County's Lake Machado, "gator wranglers" were hired by the city officials to apprehend him. How long could Reggie hold out?

His sorry plight began when two men, one a former LA police officer, decided Reggie had outgrown the backyard pond that he reluctantly shared with three other reptiles. The time had come, they thought, to dump him in the lake. That was in August of 2005. Shortly afterward, they were arrested for illegally raising exotic animals.

Once Reggie was spotted by gathering crowds, he became an overnight sensation, setting off ripples all the way to Europe! What a bizarre place to find an alligator anyway; this wasn't Florida or Louisiana. The locals decided to call him Reggie, allowing him a kind of "folk hero" aura.

Reggie might have had a chance to escape if those "city officials" had not cordoned off the entire fifty-three-acre lake. Reggie had managed to elude capture for nearly three months from those "gator wrestlers." He began to make fewer and fewer appearances "until he seemed to disappear altogether."

For nearly eighteen months, there were no further sightings of Reggie. He was thought to be dead or hibernating. It was at this time, before his death, that Steve Irwin, the "Crocodile Hunter," announced that he and his crew would attempt to capture him should he reemerge.

It isn't likely Reggie considered Irwin's announcement a challenge, but he finally reappeared on April 30, 2007, at least a foot longer since his last sighting. Even more specialists were contacted now to "try and bring him in." Reggie wasn't basking in all the "media attention," but about 3:30 p.m. on May 24, 2007, he emerged from the water and made his way over to a three-hundred--foot dry spot to "bask in the sun," which is exactly what alligators enjoy doing.

But time was running out for Reggie. Officials and wildlife experts were hovering nearby to once and for all "find a way to snag the gator," judged to be about twenty years old and seven feet long. When the opportunity presented itself, they cornered him, wrestling to restrain the thrashing Reggie. At this moment, Ian Recchio, curator of reptiles and amphibians at the Los Angeles Zoo, "jumped on his back, threw a t-shirt over his head and wrapped duct tape around his snout."

By this time, Reggie had experienced a true "Hollywood" type capture swarmed by fans and photographers. He was whisked away in an animal control truck by police escort, after fire fighters had strapped him to a board. Adding to the drama were the TV helicopters flying over the rush hour freeway journey, broadcasting live footage along the way. By the time of his capture, Reggie had cost the city $200,000, but Angelenos were rewarded with fond memories and shared stories that united them as strangers. T-shirts and songs about Reggie ensued.

Is this the end of the story? Stay tuned. Reggie had "big plans" after he arrived at the LA Zoo. But first he had to be quarantined for thirty to sixty days, Recchio stated. Then he would be introduced into a pool with other alligators, which could take weeks.

Once Reggie had settled into his pen with his new "pals," it didn't take him long to size up his surroundings. By this time, he may have become weary of all the attention and visitors. But for whatever reason, on August 15, 2007, Reggie decided to "make a break for it" and escaped from his pen. After zookeepers discovered he was missing, the hunt was on. He was later found near a loading dock within the zoo proper, and returned to his cage.

Modifications to his habitat were definitely in order. By May 10, 2010, Reggie had moved into a "new gator pond" near the zoo's entrance. His body size had increased to 7'6", weighing 118 pounds. Every week he eats two to three pounds of assorted meats—chicken, fish, rats, or specially formulated alligator chow with vitamin supplements. And across the street, his own cafe, Reggie's Bistro, provides savory selections for his visitors, including the Reggie burger.

So for the southeastern transplant to Southern California, Reggie is thriving amidst all his fellow Angelenos. Way to go Reggie!

The North American Alligator

Alligators are unique in many ways. They have changed little during their existence on earth for over two hundred million years. This is largely due to a variety of "successful adaptations" they have maintained, such as breaking their prey into small pieces and swallowing them, instead of chewing, allowing the stones contained in their gizzards (stomach) to grind up food and aid digestion.

North American Alligators, native to wetlands throughout the Southeastern United States, have large, slightly rounded bodies with thick limbs, broad heads and powerful tails, growing to a size of 7–14'. They are carnivorous and enjoy crabs, fish, frogs, snakes, and raccoons. Their stealth-like abilities can be attributed to the location of the eyes, ears, and nostrils on top of the head, allowing them to "see, hear, and breathe while almost submerged in water." Does the image of a surfacing submarine come to mind? And would you also wonder how they can catch prey underwater without getting water in their lungs, and possibly drowning? This is due to another special adaptation to their mouth which allows this advantage.

Fortunately, alligators are no longer listed as an endangered species and are protected by the "combined efforts of federal and state wildlife agencies."

The list of unique features of the North American alligator is extensive and worth further reading on: EN.Wikipedia.org/wiki/American-Alligator.

Bibliography

KTLA.com/news/landing/ktla-reggie-alligator-new home

FoxNews.com—LA's Reggie the alligator captured, taken to zoo

Los Angeles Zoo.
lazoo.org.animals/reptiles/namerican alligator.

Environmental Conservation Online System.
ecos.fws.gov/speciesprofilefloridaconservation.org/gators

Louisana Alligator Advisory Council.
Alligatorfur.com/alligator.

Lachman, Robert. High-resolution images, August 16 and 17, 2007. Copyright, 2016, *Los Angeles Times*. Reprinted with permission.

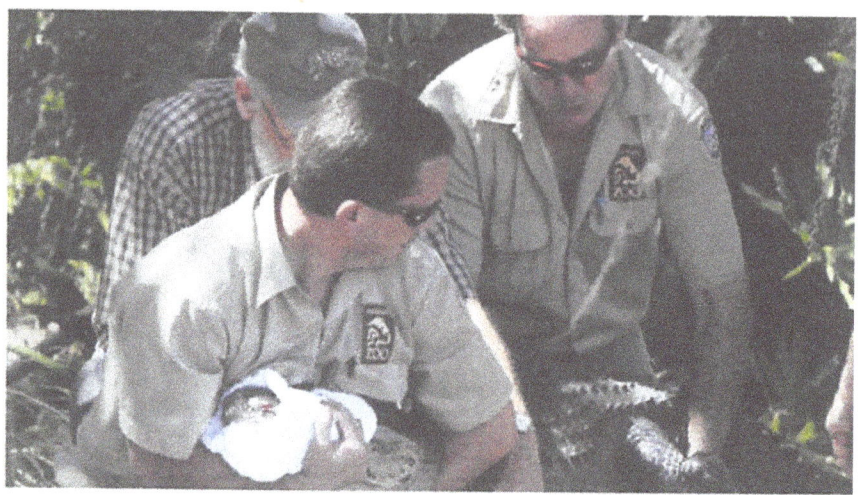

See you later, alligator: Reggie's handler, Ian Recchio, grips the alligator's powerful jaws after his capture, May 24, 2007.

Reggie in his pen near the zoo entrance—doing his favorite thing

Roaming no more: Reggie at his new home in the Los Angeles Zoo after his capture, May 24, 2007

Marching Off to Solitary, August 16, 2007

Reggie the alligator— the John Dillinger of semiaquatic reptiles—was returned to custody Wednesday after having busted out of the slammer at the LA Zoo overnight.

Dolphins Lead the Way

Far below the sea, near the Hotel del Coronado, an Atlantic bottlenose dolphin navigates along rocky, sandy areas in a routine mission for the Space and Naval Warfare System Pacific Center. What he discovers is not on the program.

The dolphin Spetz has discovered an object on the ocean floor and surfaces from the shallow-water dive to touch the front of the boat—meaning he has found something. Spetz is then ordered to take the marker, consisting of a small weight with a float, and leave it where the object was found. It is a remarkable find of the second known Howell torpedo in existence. One treasure has found another.

Chris Harris, a veteran of thirty years' experience with marine mammals, is operations supervisor for the bioscience division at the Navy's Point Loma facility in San Diego and has observed many dives. "The bottlenose dolphin is highly trainable, adaptable, and shows great strength in the marine environment. They are cared for by a talented group of marine mammal veterinarians who work hand-in-glove with the Animal Training Staff." These two groups are responsible for channeling dolphins into becoming the equivalent of aquanauts of the sea.

Spetz works with human partners who train him using positive reinforcement (correct responses are rewarded and incorrect responses are ignored). It normally takes seven years to train a dolphin for deep water recovery. "Dolphins are trained in the ocean and return at the end of the day to their bay homes at the naval base," Chris comments. "This allows them to socialize with other dolphins."

When Spetz discovered the Howell torpedo, he was demonstrating two key elements of his unique nature-sensory and diving capabilities. His sensory capabilities provide the most sophisticated sonar system known to man that no manmade technology can equal. And with his diving capabilities, in both shallow and deep water, his exceptional eyesight allows him to peer into dark, murky water and detect objects of various shapes that human divers have difficulty finding.

To ensure dolphins like Spetz are kept healthy and fit, the navy continues its tradition of studying marine mammal nutrition, medicine, physiology, and environmental ecology. A full-time staff of veterinarians and technicians are ready to respond around the clock, seven days a week. Maintaining the health of marine mammals is the primary mission of the navy's Marine Mammal Program.

Of equal importance are a dolphin's sonar abilities. Sonar, or sound navigation, uses sound to detect the location of underwater objects. Sonar technology sends out sounds and waits for their response after bouncing off an object—possibly an explosive undersea mine.

As Spetz enters the water during a morning run, he makes clicking sounds while he maneuvers underwater. He has activated his bio-sonar skill to target any object he may encounter; listening for echoes when the sound hits an object. This sonar process is called echolocation. It allows him to tell the difference between a BB gun and a kernel of corn—his sense of hearing is that precise.

The echolocation is a complicated process and involves a dolphin's nasal passage and forehead to beam the sound into the water. The returning echo passes through fat in the jaw to the inner ear, activating nerve impulses in the brain to interpret an object's size, shape, and material. Scientists do not fully understand how a dolphin's brain interprets this sonar information. It translates into the idea of "seeing objects with our ears," which is what dolphins do. By studying them, we may someday improve our own sonar technology.

Spetz has a playful side to his nature as well. He uses sound to communicate to fellow dolphins with squeaks and whistles from the blowhole on the top of his head, along with sending sound through his body leaping into the air and slapping his tail into the water. His eating habits are fairly simple. "He only eats fish of restaurant quality," Chris comments. "And swallow's his food whole instead of chewing it."

The research programs at the navy's Marine Mammal Program are unsurpassed. Every day they conduct development of systems and technology to learn more about marine mammals—areas such as sensory systems, hydrodynamics, anatomy and physiology, healthcare, behavior, reproduction, and sea operations.

Animal health includes developing artificial insemination to improve genetic diversity worldwide and the possible use of dolphins to monitor the environmental conditions of the world's oceans. The development of a biosonar measurement tool will allow a dolphin-wearable computer to collect emitted clicks and returning echo's for further evaluation. Eventually, hardware sonar systems will perform as well as the dolphin. The Navy's Dolphin Breeding Program is necessary for the replacement of aging dolphins with their young who will participate in more advanced training methods. All dolphins' young have been born at the naval facility since 1988.

On that day back in May of 2013, one treasure from the nineteenth century was found by another from the twenty-first century, each in its own existence, marking their unique spots in history. The Howell torpedo was the first torpedo to target its object without leaving a trail of turbulence behind. The bottlenose dolphin acts as a quasi-torpedo with its unique biosonar system. Both enhanced the world around them.

The Bottlenose Dolphin–
Up Close and Personal

The bottlenose dolphin has a certain celebrity attached to it—marine parks, movies, and television programs. But their down to earth environment starts with the temperate and tropical oceans they inhabit throughout the world. They maintain a wide genetic diversity. Their snout serves as a blowhole on top of their heads and their necks are more flexible than other dolphins-only two of their seven vertebrae are fused.

They're sociable mammals and live in groups of fifteen on average. They enjoy a diet of eels, squids, shrimp, and a wide variety of fish, swallowing their food whole. They search for prey by using a sonar type system—sending out sounds and listening for return echoes. This helps them to determine the location and shape of close encounters.

The bottlenose dolphins are highly intelligent and interact well with humans—hence their proclivity as performance animals and as participants in US Navy Marine Mammal Programs. But more restrictions are needed to prevent harmful human interactions when dolphins are accidently killed as a "by catch of tuna fishing."

Bibliography

Harris, Christian, Operations Supervisor of Navy's Marine Mammal Program.
San Diego. Interviewed August 12, 3013.

Hot Stuff Works, "How Can Dolphins Disarm Sea Mines?"
www.science.howstuffworks.com/zoology marine-life/dolphins-disarm.

Navy Marine Mammal Program.
www.public-navy.mil/spawar/pacific/71500/page/default/aspx

Perry, Tony, "Navy Dolphins Discover Rare Old Torpedo off Coronado.
Los Angeles Times, May 17, 2013.

Wikipedia, "Common Bottle Nose Dolphins."
www.en.wikipedia.org/wiki/common_bottlenose_dolphin

US Navy Photo by Photographer's Mate First Class Brien Aho, March 2013.

US Navy Photo by Mass Communication Specialist Second Class David Cothran,
May 2013.

AP Photo/SSC Pacific, US Navy. Permitted release from NBC Universal, KNSD.

Bottlenose Dolphin

This hero dolphin from the 715 Marine Mammal Team discovered a nineteenth-century Howell torpedo off San Diego last year, 2013.

This Howell torpedo at the Naval Undersea Museum in Keyport, Wash, was thought to be the only one in existence, but Navy trained dolphins found another one in the ocean off Coronado (US Navy)

US Navy Howell Torpedo discovered by Dolphins March 2013 during a routine exercise. Torpedo will undergo extensive restoration.

Armed dolphin trained by US navy to kill terrorists..

The Surfing Fish

It's late at night, close to midnight, with a full June moon beckoning. The ocean has begun to swell near shore followed by a crest of waves carrying thousands of silvery creatures to the edge of the beach. The grunion have landed.

By taking a closer look at these "little fish," we learn their spawning season is from March through August, peaking in April through June, and covering an area from Baja along the Gulf Coast to Santa Barbara along the Pacific Coast. They arrive under a full moon in sync with the high tides, spawning several hours from two to four nights. Grunion are exceptional in that they are found nowhere else in the world; a unique California coast experience and adventure.

Once the female is beached, she finds the damp sand that provides a natural, protective environment to house her eggs. She reaches as far up the slope as possible and proceeds to arch her back, keeping her head up, while digging out the damp sand with her tail. She continues digging out a trench while twisting her body until she is buried up to her pectoral fins, depositing her eggs four inches below the surface.

After settling into her nest, up to eight males attempt to mate by curving around her and releasing their milt, which then flows down her body until it reaches the eggs to fertilize them. Once spawning has occurred, the males head for the ocean, their night of frolicking over. Nature allows grunion to stay in the sand fifteen to twenty minutes because of their ability to slow their metabolism to use less oxygen. This allows the female time to twist free and return to the sea on the next wave. The eggs are left to incubate in the sand without being immersed in seawater. Normally there is a window of time, from ten to fourteen days, for them to hatch before the next series of high tides have a chance to reach them. But another twist of nature surrounds the eggs' survival. The seawater and the agitation of the rising surf trigger the hatching which takes place in less than one minute. It is this unique spawning behavior that attracts participants and exclamations of "I don't believe it!"

Considering the length of the spawning season, females spawn about six times during a season laying up to eighteen eggs. The term "mighty grunion" is aptly applied. But not to be outdone, the milt from the male sperm can produce as many as one million sperm with several spawning per run. All that activity from a "little fish" whose normal size is six to seven inches. According to Karen Martin, PhD, "it is not clear where grunion go when not spawning; they may migrate deeper under the sea in winter."

As we look more closely into the daily lives of the grunion we find that they have no teeth and live from three to four years. They feed on very small organisms such as Plankton, and have more than their share of predators. These include larger fish, shore birds such as egrets and herons, along with seagulls, sea lions and sand sharks, sand worms and beetles. So the little grunion face many challenges, including reduction of spawning areas due to beach erosion, harbor construction and pollution. In addition, pipeline breaks from oil drilling cause oil spills to end up on shore that is bad for all beach animals and affects potential spawning habitats. Clean-up crews try to use cleaning by hand and continue to observe the beaches for the next grunion run.

While fishing is allowed a license is required, but restricted from use from April through June when peak spawning time for grunion occurs. During the remaining months, observers are encouraged to "catch and release." The California Department of Fish and Games weighs in by prohibiting the use of gear, traps or nets. In addition, the Beach Ecology Coalition holds annual meetings to address such beach protocol and encourage use of their motto "observe and conserve."

Throughout history, grunion have contributed to California culture and fascination. The early coastal Indians harvested grunion from their own "grunion runs." Centuries later, archeologists found fossil remains at various Indian campsites, dating to four thousand years ago during the Pleistocene age. The first scientific description of a grunion spawning was in 1916, a hundred years ago. And today, grunion continue to thrive and enchant their observers.

The Grunion Greeters

The "little fish" have much to be proud of in all the interest they create at the beach and beyond. The most formidable of their protectors are the "Grunion Greeters." Established in 2002, they grew out of the concern of a group of trained volunteers in San Diego, consisting of scientists, community members, environmental organizations, surfers, and beach workers. These "citizen scientists" foresaw the need for beach grooming practices, and planning future beach restoration and policies for grunion runs. In this way they can better understand the habits and habitats of the grunion. They also join forces with researchers from NOAA (National Oceanic and Atmospheric Administration) to track grunion fish population.

During the first few months of "run season," the Grunion Greeters stand on the beach observing fish activities and recording for NOAA records, along with their own science project. It should also be noted that the grunion run schedule is posted in a California publication for the open seasons of March, June, July and August. Volunteers are encouraged to attend workshops for preparation of monitoring beach-spawning populations.

As you can see, the grunion hold a special place in the hearts of their followers, and along with music, art, film, and television, they continue to inspire. Thanks for sharing "little fish."

BIBLIOGRAPHY

"From Here to Eternity: Grunion Put on a Show," *Los Angeles Times*, June 16, 2011.

"California Grunion Facts," California Department of Fish and Game, www.dfg.ca.gov.

Sepkoski, Jack (2002). "A compendium of fossil marine animal genera."
Bulletins of American Paleontology 364: p. 560

Julianne E. Steers/grunion.org.
provided high-resolution images

Up close and personal

A Grunion gathering

On the beach

Grunion eggs at one week before hatching—
you can see their eyes.

The Case of the Stowaway Albatross

An albatross does not usually hitch a ride on a pickup truck, but one did after traveling thousands of miles on a cargo ship across the Pacific. This is a rare event in California.

After the truck driver released the Laysan albatross to a nearby Lifeguard station at Cabrillo Beach, it was handed over to Julie Skoglund, manager of International Bird Rescue Wildlife Center in San Pedro. "They are such amazing creatures, very independent and almost seeming tame, but it's more that their demeanor is calm," Julie says. Julie was instrumental in rescue work after the Gulf oil spill, going on to design and build an oiled bird center in Alabama, and managing bird care in Louisiana.

The Laysan remained at the Wildlife Center for four days under the expert care of Julie and her staff, consisting of an intern and two to six volunteers a day. "Laysan do not eat well in captivity," Julie comments, "and generally if they are healthy, like the one we had, they can go long periods of time without food. With the Laysan that we had in care, it received two to three tubings of a special fish based elemental diet at 5 percent of its body weight. So we fill syringes with this diet in liquid form and attach a long tube that we put down the birds esophagus into its gizzard. This Laysan was fortunate, as it was in great condition when it arrived," Julie continues, "meaning it had no injuries, was within normal body weight and had normal blood values."

If the Laysan was in such good health, this brings to question why the bird had to be kept for four days. "We kept it for four days," Julie states, "to ensure it was waterproof and to coordinate a boat release. Many of these birds come in with feathers contaminated from being on various substrate (environmental impacts) and we want to always make sure they are released in prime condition."

How exactly the Laysan became a stowaway is a bit of a mystery. If only the bird could talk. "We have no idea how this bird got into the back of the truck," Julie remarks. "Either it landed there in an attempt to land or someone just found it and put it back there."

What is particularly fascinating about this seabird is the aero dynamics it displays as it soars high above the ocean to ride the ocean winds. Sometimes it glides for hours without rest or flapping its wings. According to Julie, "Birds have the ability to use one-half of their brain at a time while sleeping. Laysan also have a special mechanism in their wing so they can lock their wings while soaring, therefore expending little to no energy while flying. This enables them to travel extremely long distances with very little caloric expenditures and to sleep on the wing." Albatross sail on the wind and fly into the wind to gain elevation, and then turn back toward the sea to gain speed. They are more gliders than flyers.

Laysan have been known to live up to sixty years and weigh up to twenty-five pounds. Being a surface feeder, it feeds on anything that floats on the ocean's surface, namely squid, fish crustaceans, and flying fish eggs. Feeding mostly at night, it grabs its prey from just under the surface of the water.

After the bird received a clean bill of health, it was ready to be released. Taking special care, Julie scooped it out of its aquatic enclosure with a net and wrapped it in a beach towel. Once it received a final examination, she fitted it with a metal ID band before putting it in a crate. Julie has high expectations that they will receive band reports on the Laysan.

True to its form, the Laysan "honked, fidgeted, and snapped its long beak" as staffers loaded it into a city lifeguard boat for its ride back to Cabrillo Beach. After the bird was tossed into the water, it shook off, and stretched its wings. It took only ten seconds before it skittered across the water, flapping its wings, and flew into the sky toward the horizon. "We want it to go back and be a successful part of the breeding population," Julie said. The journey across the ocean was expected to take only a few days. Can you picture it now soaring over the Mid-Pacific?

Conservation Efforts for Laysan Albatross

Of the twenty species of albatross recognized, nineteen are threatened with extinction. Although the Laysan is considered a more common species, conservation efforts are vital to its existence. Plastic debris that wash into the sea is picked up by the parents, who in turn feed it to their chick. This causes the chick to lose weight or even starve to death. The bait used for long-line fishing attracts seabirds for feeding, causing them to become hooked on the line and drown. As a consequence of these threats and others, governments, conservation organizations, and the fishing industry are all cooperating in finding solutions to protect seabird populations and their breeding colonies.

Breeding habits of Laysan Albatross

Laysan albatross gather in large colonies to breed on islands in the Mid-Pacific Hawaiian chain from November through July. Before actual breeding takes place, the male performs a series of elaborate dance movements and bonds with a mate for life. This allows the pair to "cooperatively" raise their young.

The nests they build are from simple scoops of sand and available vegetation. By mid-November the female is ready to lay her single white egg, which both parents take turns incubating. When the chick hatches after two months, it must rely on the parents to obtain food. Once they return with food from the sea, they feed the chick by regurgitating rich, oily squid that sustains it for several days. Five to six months after hatching, the chick is left on its own. It will spend three to five years at sea before returning to its nesting colony in search of a mate.

Bibliography

Barbosa, Tony. "A Seafaring Bird Visits LA." *Los Angeles Times*, February 1, 2012

Laysan Albatross (http://sailhawaii.com/alba.html) (Accessed 7/24/2012).

Laysan Albatross & Plastics (www.monteraybayacquarium.org/oceanissues/plastics-albatross) (Accessed 7/24/2012).

Midway Atoll National Wildlife Refuge
www.fws.gov/midway/laal.hml (Accessed 7/24/2012).

National Geographic, www.nationalgeographic.com/animals/birds/albatross
(Accessed 7/24/2012).

Nature Works Laysan Albatross, www.nhptv.ore/natureworks/laysan.htm (Accessed 7/24/2012).

Safina, Carl. "On the Wings of the Albatross." National Geographic (December 2007, 86-1 13).

Skoglund, Julie, Manager, International Bird Rescue Wildlife Waystation/Los Angeles Interviewed October 8, 2012. www.wildlifewaystation.org.

Chamberlin, Bob. High-resolution images, May 12, 2012. "Copyright, 2016, *Los Angeles Times*. Reprinted with Permission."

The Laysan Albatross

The albatross rides in its carrying case in the back of a Los Angeles City lifeguard boat on its way back to life in the wild.

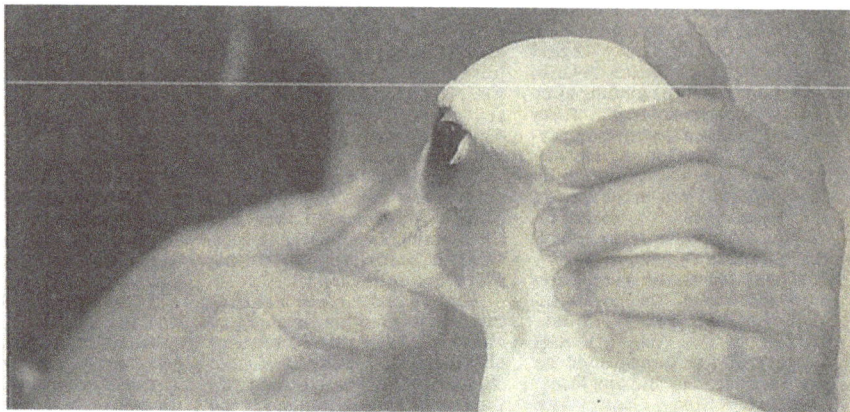

JULIE SKOGLUND GIVES the bird a final examination and fits it with a metal identification band as she prepares it for release after four days of rest and relaxation.

AFTER A RESTFUL few days of hanging out at a San Pedro wildlife rescue facility, the albatross is taken to sea and released by International bird rescue manager Julie Skoglund, *rear*, and Adam Ribota

TAGGED SO THAT IT can be identified again, the albatross sets off on its next journey, heading for the horizon as its rescuers cheer it on.

A Tale of Two Wolves

The wolves are speaking to us; especially two distinct wolves who need us to listen as they weave their own tales. Both have a rendezvous with history by their unique involvement with nature. They need us to understand.

On December 28, 2011, a lone gray wolf trots across the border from northeastern Oregon into Siskiyou County, California–the first documented wild wolf in nearly ninety years. State and federal biologists waste no time in attaching a tracking collar to OR7, his official designation.

He zigzags over three thousand miles crossing through forests and sub-lands, up and down mountains and across rural highways in northeast California. This "lonely lobo," averaging fifty miles a day, marks places along the way which he revisits in 2013.

He finds enough prey in Elk and Deer on relatively sparce land, but not the mate he is searching for. Wolves are incredibly social animals. We don't know what is on his mind, but he decides to cross back over into Oregon between March and April of 2012, staying for thirty days before returning to revisit some of his earlier sites. With his homing abilities he can find the same locations returning from a completely different direction. He likes what he sees in California but decides to make his final exit in March of 2013, crossing again into Oregon.

Several hundred miles south, towards San Diego, California our journey takes us to the other wolf in our narrative–the sub-species known as the Mexican gray wolf. At one time they numbered in the hundreds of thousands, but were reduced to just a few by the 1960's. Poisoning, shootings, even federal rewards, brought them precariously close to extinction.

Fortunately, there exists many managed facilities in the southwest, and now protected under California's Endangered Species Act. One such facility is the California Wolf Center in Julian near San Diego. According to Christina Souto, associate director of Development and Communications, the facility "acts as a breeding and housing center, and is one of the largest institutions hosting Mexican gray wolves in the world."

The Mexican Wolf Species Survival Plan, which manages about three hundred captive wolves in the US and Mexico, allows for breeding in several facilities and reintroduction into the southwest. It is possible that someday a pack of Mexican gray wolves, released into the wilderness, could join the over one hundred Mexican wolves already roaming in protected areas in New Mexico and Arizona. The President of California's Fish and Game Commission, Michael Sutton, stated "there is no more iconic animal in the American west than this one. We owe it to them to do everything we can to help them re-colonize their historic range in our state."

This brings us to the Mexican gray wolf in our story, known by his tag name as M863, who is a prime example of both the Mexican Survival Plan and the California Wolf Center. Christina Souto comments, "M863 was born at the Sevilleta National Wildlife Refuge on April 5th, 2004 and released into the wild at three months of age. Unfortunately, he was brought back into captivity due to depredation, but continues to play a critical role in the Mexican survival plan. His face has a very distinguished look, matched only by his distinguished personality. He is one of the largest Mexican gray wolves at the California Wolf Center."

When M863 arrived at the CWC in 2008, he naturally became a part of their important breeding program to increase the population of his sub-species. As a result, he helps support the reintroduction of these wolves in the wild to become the "lobos" of the southwest. As Christina once more comments, "he is an amazing dad and has been seen taking care of, guarding, and playing with his pups. M863 has a favorite rock in his habitat that he loves to stand on and look out to guard his pack."

The California Wolf Center provides a sustainable population management plan which includes the use of genetic diversity to avoid inbreeding. Erin Hunt, General Manager of the CWC comments thoughtfully, "conservation centers like ours have a role to play by giving people opportunities to learn that wolves are not aggressive and blood-thirsty, as they are often portrayed. Instead, they are highly intelligent, social animals with family structures not unlike our own. If people can see this firsthand, they are more likely to make a personal connection with these incredible animals and invest in protecting them in the wild so that wolves remain for generations to come." Wolves truly add a sense of home to the land they occupy.

   As we rejoin OR7, to further enhance his journey, we see he has made his way south to the Oregon Cascades, far away from wolf packs in northeastern Oregon where he was born in the spring of 2009. The founding members of his Imnala pack had originally migrated from Idaho, but by 2011 OR7 left his pack to find territory and a mate–the embodiment of the "mythic" lone wolf. He made the right decision to avoid Idaho in his quest, as the pacific coast may be the only area in the US where wolves can survive and thrive.

   By May of 2014, OR7 was closing in on finding a mate in the Rogue River-Siskiyou National Forest. Images of him with a black female wolf in the same area were found by wildlife biologists who were monitoring with remote cameras. Indeed, by this time it was believed the pair had denned and were rearing their two pups, now known as the Rogue pack. This was an eventful episode as it marked the first known wolf breeding in the Oregon Cascades since the early twentieth century.

   John Stephenson, a biologist for the US Fish and Wildlife Service, works closely with Oregon biologists and has been monitoring OR7. "It always seemed like a real long shot that he'd find a female wolf in the same area," he stated. There aren't any." They don't know where the female came from or that she would find him so far away from where most wolves are. As of May, 2015 the celebrated pair have added three more pups to their pack–the Rogue pack 7.

THE ANIMAL CONNECTION

John Stephenson summed up his view of OR7 by stating, "He has been a fascinating story—a very special wolf. We've learned a lot about wolf dispersing from what he's done."

As we look back on the compelling lives of OR7 and M863, we can appreciate the commitment each has made to further enhance our understanding of the wolf story. Much work remains in protecting them as free ranging animals and in educating the public, so that a coordinated effort can be achieved. We've heard their story.

The Protection of Wolves and Their Biodiversity

The two most important issues facing wolves today are advancing their recovery through greater human tolerance and utilizing the wolves' ability to practice "biodiversity."

In sharing the landscape with wolves, we allow their recovery program to endure. Livestock depredation can be controlled by use of permanent or portable fencing, cloth flags placed at intervals along a fence, installation of motion sensors around sensitive areas and use of livestock guard dogs to warn of approaching wolves. Such measures provide the conservation solutions needed to forge a successful co-existence between wolves and humans.

Wolves help to balance the ecosystems they occupy by becoming "engineers of biodiversity." The wolf is the dominate predator, and as his species dwindles, the coyote population explodes leaving the foxes and badgers to compete for smaller game—so they dwindle. Large Elk also increase in population, stripping the landscape of vegetation and the streams of side covers of aspen and willow. In addition, there exist few scraps from the wolves killings for scavenger magpies, ravens and grizzly bears. The diversified ecosystem that wolves provide are part of the symbiotic relationship that has existed for thousands of years. On a more hopeful note, Federal Wildlife Service are helping to establish coexistence workshops for livestock owners in Montana.

Bibliography

Hunt, Erin, General Manager of the California Wolf Center/Julian, CA

Souto, Christina, Associate Director of Development and Communications of the California Wolf Center/Julian, CA.

Nature's Voice, NRDC, Fall 2015.
www.nrdc.org.

Stephenson, John, Biologist US Fish and Wildlife Service/Oregon Interviewed October 9, 2014.

Boxwall, Betina. "Wolf Likes State But Is Unlikely To Find Love." *Los Angeles Times*, January 2, 2013.

High-resolution images courtesy of US Fish and Wildlife Service, John Stephinson, Biologist, and the California Wolf Center.

Two of wolf OR7 pups peek out from log on the Rogue River-Siskiyou National Forest, June 2, 2014. Photo courtesy of US Fish and Wildlife Service.

OR7, caught by remote cameras in the Oregon Cascades, May 2014.

M863 in Captivity.

Jumping for joy!

M863—proud father.

Outfoxing Extinction

At first glance, the Catalina Island fox seems to have an easy life with enough to eat and no known predators. But in 1999 this fox was near extinction. We need to take a closer look.

The Catalina Island, one of eight Channel Islands, is located about thirty miles off the coast of Southern California. Based on limited fossil records, the Catalina Island fox may have lived on the island from 800 to 3,800 years ago. Collaborative research conducted by archaeologists Renee Vallanoweth and Torben Rick used carbon dating of several fox skeletons found on the Channel Islands. Dr. Vallanoweth believes that the foxes were brought to the islands by "indigenous people," carried over from the mainland as they began to establish settlements. The Catalina Island fox represents one of six subspecies of fox, each unique to the island it lives on.

The Catalina Island includes grasslands, dunes, coastal bluffs, with hills and canyons dotted by sage, cactus and island Chaparral. Its geographic isolation resulted in a lack of immunity to parasites and disease brought in from the mainland. By 1999, the fox population was ravaged by a distemper epidemic, most likely caused by a pet dog or raccoon from the mainland. Before this occurrence, the fox population numbered 1,300.

Close to extinction, the little fox needed human help to "outfox extinction." Thanks to the Catalina Island conservancy and its partner, the Institute of Wildlife Studies, the Catalina Island Recovery Plan was implemented. Feral pigs were removed, the golden-eagle relocated, a vaccination program established to protect against canine distemper and wild fox population monitored. Weekly visits by a pilot, accompanied by a wildlife biologist, allow a plane to fly over the island to track nearly sixty foxes equipped with telemetry collars.

The Catalina Island fox is possibly the smallest fox in North America, weighing four to six pounds, about the size of a house cat. Its small size is an adaptation to the limited resources available in the island environment. It is more colorful than its larger gray fox descendant on the mainland, with a gray body, pointed nose, reddish ears and feet and black tipped tail. Due to the restrictions of the island, the foxes do not migrate.

The island fox typically mates for life and are seen together starting in January and through to early March. In captivity the island fox can live eight to ten years. They enjoy fruits, insects, birds, crabs, lizards, and small mammals, including deer mice.

If we were to follow the "wildlife technicians" at daybreak on the island, we would see them strode through waist-high brush, inspecting the contents of twelve wire-box traps baited the night before with kibble and cat food. The trapped fox has a mask applied to calm it down while it receives treatment to keep it healthy. At this juncture, wildlife biologists take over to inspect the foxes for illnesses, vaccinate them, fit them with telemetry collars and monitor their behavior.

Because of the hard work the conservationists practiced to achieve their goals, the Catalina Island fox achieved one of the most remarkable recoveries known for an endangered species. In just thirteen years, they went from a population of 100 to 1,542. It is hoped that continued monitoring and protection will lead to their eventual removal from the endangered species list.

Conservation—It's All About Protection

Thanks to the establishment of the Catalina Island Fox Recovery Plan, vaccinations, captive breeding (now eliminated), along with contained monitoring, the fox population has increased to what it is today—over 1,500 foxes. But beyond these more direct approaches of protection, lie the Catalina Island itself and the thousands of tourists it attracts, not to mention the over four thousand residents who live there.

Catalina Island lies twenty-two miles southwest of Los Angeles and could almost be imagined as a capsule of Hawaiian allure. There is north Catalina with its town of Two Harbors—picture underwater diving, boating and camping. And the even more compelling city of Avalon in the south, with palm trees and cabanas along Descanso Beach. The circular, art deco Catalina Casino is the cultural center with a movie theater and museum. In between these two cities there are chair lifts across the island and numerous tours—you can actually observe a herd of 150 bison—thirty left over from the filming of a silent Hollywood movie.

With all the island activities and sights to see, there is a continued danger the little fox faces—vehicle trauma. This is the number one cause of fox mortalities. To counter this, the Conservancy has erected signs to warn motorists that foxes are present. A radar speed sign is used for readings of vehicles going over 25 mph, especially in early morning and dusk. As a society, we need to realize how important it is to respect their space.

Bibliography

Catalina Island Conservancy, "Foxes."
HTTP://www.catalinaconservancy.org/index.

Center for Biological Diversity, "Natural History."
HTTP://www.biologicaldiversity.org/species/mammals/island fox.

Collins, P.W. "Interaction between the island foxes and Indians off the coast of Southern California." *Journal of Ethnobiology* 11:51-82.

Gilbert, D.A. et al. "Genetic fingerprinting reflects population differentiation in the California Channel Island fox." Nature 344(6268):764-767.

Sahagun, Louis (2012-01-19). "Catalina island fox makes astounding comeback."
HTTP://www.latimes.com/news/local/la-me-fox-20120l19

Chamberlin, Bob. High-resolution images, January 19, 2012. "Copyright, 2016, *Los Angeles Times*. Reprinted with permission."

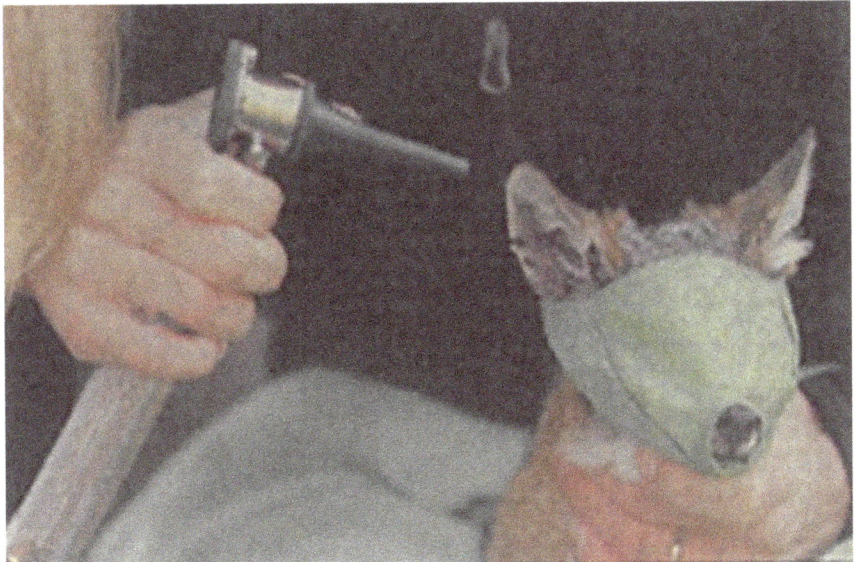

A TRAPPED FOX has a mask on to keep it calm while it receives treatment to keep it healthy.

A CATALINA ISLAND FOX awaits the attentions of biologists who trap the animals so they can inspect them for illnesses, vaccinate them, outfit them with telemetry collars and monitor their behavior.

WILDLIFE BIOLOGIST Julie King gets ready to examine one of the foxes trapped overnight.

Project Wildlife

Have you ever thought about what happens to all nature's creatures who are injured and sick out in the wilderness? Where do they go? Who can take care of them? Wild animals who are injured and sick can often become debilitated and end up wherever people find them, sometimes hidden away. But most are not found and many eaten by predators.

Some lucky animals may be rescued and cared for at a rehab facility called "Project Wildlife." Established in 1972, this is one of the largest rehabilitation organizations in the United States. Located in San Diego, California, it helps over ten thousand wild creatures a year. The rehab program provides trained Satellite Care Volunteers to nurture animals until their release. The volunteers work on teams that go through specialized training for their particular animal, and are equipped with all the supplies they need.

While most animals are returned to their habitats in the wild, there are some who serve as "wildlife ambassadors" and like nothing better than to share their stories and remain in the satellite homes of their caregivers. The animal ambassadors are presented at a variety of programs—schools, scout, and community groups such as libraries, nature centers, churches and private parties. The caregivers take the animals to these functions, or specially trained presenters pick them up and return them to their caregivers.

According to Trish Jackman, Wildlife Rehabilitation manager, "The satellite care program's goal is to rehab and release. But we can't release an animal that is not 100 percent capable of survival. However, occasionally we have one that would do well in a captive environment."

The ambassador animals form a mosaic of experiences, each with special needs that prevent them from being released back into the wilderness, such as Boo, a young owl who was hand-raised and unable to protect himself. Since Boo has formed a special bond with his caregiver, he makes mating calls to let the caregiver know that he's his chosen mate.

Once Trish has selected which animals will serve as ambassadors she considers the best candidates for education. After the wildlife veterinarian does an exam, they select the qualified candidates, find a proper caregiver, and go through a complicated permit process.

Trish has been in the animal field for nineteen years in various endeavors, working with everything from hippos to bats. She has had the opportunity to know most of the ambassadors and brought many on board. "I am responsible for their medical, husbandry, and training. I also determine if a potential rehab animal that can't be released would be a good candidate for education. Working with the education manager allows me to identify the best housing/caregiver for a new animal, and advise the education manager on appropriate handlers for the animal."

One particular ambassador Trish especially connected with is Bobber the Kestrel—a falcon who bobs his head up and down. "He came to us as a juvenile with an eye injury. The technician felt he should go home with me for extra care and monitoring. As the eye healed, I noticed that he was very calm with other younger Kestrels." Upon further examination, Trish noticed a slight indentation in his skull. The veterinarian confirmed he had suffered head trauma and a brain injury.

During the one year Bobber lived with Trish he was trained to sit on a glove and not kept isolated the way a rehab patient would be. He needed to be comfortable with humans. "During the time he was with me, he would greet me each morning with a trill and vocalize in a soft voice when he saw me, but would not eat his food until I returned from work at night. At that time he would enjoy his meal while I ate my dinner. The veterinarian and I soon realized that he viewed me as either his partner or parent and even though he was designed to eat during the day he would wait for me."

THE ANIMAL CONNECTION

Eventually Bobber was transferred to his current volunteer caregiver but still trills for Trish when they see each other. "Even though they are in captivity and tolerate humans, we still need to encourage those natural behaviors. Once in a while though, there is a connection that is special. Having said that, I do not pet or snuggle Bobber. He would bite me for sure."

Bobber the Kestral and Trish Jackman formed a special bond that has enhanced our understanding of the animal ambassadors. Their link to Project Wildlife is our link to knowing how they survive. Nature can open windows all around us to enjoy.

Project Wildlife's Animal Ambassadors

Bobber

Bobber came to a Project Wildlife in the summer of 2011 as a young fledgling with a head injury and was named for the way he bobs his head up and down. He couldn't be released due to neurological damage, which made him unable to reach full flight. His injuries also made him very docile and, therefore, a great animal ambassador. In addition to being a Project Wildlife animal ambassador, his tolerant nature makes him a perfect surrogate "parent" for young wild American kestrels.

Boo

Boo came to Project Wildlife as a young owl who had been raised by the public. Due to being hand-raised, Boo is not afraid of people and as a result cannot survive in the wild. Boo lives in Ramona with his caregiver with whom he has formed a special bond. In addition to flying right to his caregiver's wrist for training sessions and outings, during breeding season, Boo makes mating calls to his caregiver to let him know that he's his chosen mate!

Wildlife Extraction

Project Wildlife's mission is to improve quality of life for local wildlife through animal rescue, rehabilitation, and education. But an important ingredient of this program is provided by their wildlife extraction for the community—a new approach to pest control.

All kinds of creatures can invade your house, from bats, to opossums, to owls in your attic. And Project Wildlife's Extraction program offers a fee-based service committed to the humane treatment of wildlife. The right techniques are used to evict wildlife and establish re-entry prevention.

The program provides the following:

- Identifying the entrance
- Humane eviction of wildlife
- Cleaning or sanitizing the area
- Repair and prevention measures
- Closing up the openings
- Follow-up call or inspection
- Habitat and conservation education

This is the right approach and needs to be expanded to more communities.

Bibliography

Jackman, Trish, Wildlife Rehabilitation Manager, Project Wildlife Rehabilitation Facility/San Diego. Interviewed May 22, 2013. www.projectwildlife.orq.

Project Wildlife Ambassadors-Photo Gallery with descriptions: www.projectwildlife.orq/ambassadors
High-resolution images courtesy of project wildlife.

THE LITTLE FLYING MACHINE

Picture yourself venturing outdoors into your garden and watching a hummingbird nearby. Now take that observation one step further and imagine that same hummingbird as a "tiny aircraft" equipped with a motor, video camera, network communications and a battery. "Welcome to the future of unmanned flight."

The Pentagon has now developed a "pocket-size" drone known as the Nano Hummingbird, which represents a notable departure from the existing Nano Air Vehicles (NAV) resembling helicopters or planes. Successful flight tests in California of this "little flying machine" has paved the way for new applications of "detailed reconnaissance missions." As a mini-spy plane it will have the capability of maneuvering on the battlefield and in urban areas. According to industry insiders, the technology will allow the Nano Hummingbird to fly through open windows, sit on power lines, and capture audio and video without enemies ever knowing. However, the final version is more likely to resemble a "sparrow" whose habitat is more widespread and less likely to arouse suspicion. Defense expert Peter W. Singer has written a book on robotic warfare entitled "Wired for War." He states, "You can use these things anywhere, put them anyplace, and the target will never know they're being watched." The Pentagon's research arm, the Defense Advanced Research Projects Agency (DARPA), awarded 4 million to AeroVironment to build the Nano Hummingbird in 2006 as part of a series of experiments in nanotechnology. It proved to be a technical challenge from scratch because it pushes the limitations of aerodynamics.

The current model is a handmade prototype aircraft that emulates the flight dynamics of a hummingbird. It has a wingspan of 6.5 inches, weighs less than an AA battery, and uses only its flapping wings for propulsion and control. The hummingbird provided the best blueprint for perfecting the flapping motion that keeps the NAV in the air. The speed of its beating wings changes the thrust, which, in turn, alters the angle at which the winds can move from left to right. Applying these mechanics to the Nano Hummingbird allows it to perform precision hover flight, with a wind gust of five miles per hour, and continuous hovering for eight minutes. Further requirements include controlled transition flight, as well as rotating clockwise and counterclockwise. Managed by remote control, it also demonstrated the ability to fly outdoors to indoors and back outdoors through a normal-size doorway.

The DARPA's Nano Air Vehicle Program is leading the way for the military initiative of making one third of all its missions unmanned by 2015. AeroVironment is hopeful that the drone will be able to perform complex military missions within a decade. The success of the Nano Hummingbird was largely due to the "creative, scientific, and artistic problem-solving skills from many AV team members." They live by a philosophy of "continuous learning" supported by their unique Research and Development environment. With continuing advances in communications electronics, the size of surveillance NAV's may possibly shrink to the size of "bumblebees."

In the meantime, while you're waiting for one to fly over your garden, check out the website of AeroVironment at www.avinc.com/nano. You will have the opportunity to view the following videos:

- Outdoor/indoor flight
- Autonomous 360-degree lateral flip
- Eleven-minute endurance flight
- Precision hover flight
- Without landing gear

Enjoy all the capabilities the "little nano" has to offer. It's your future too!

How the Nano Hummingbird Got Its Name

In studying the "flight dynamics" of the hummingbird, the man-made "Nano" could not have had a better blueprint to emulate. The hummingbird has been studied intensely using wind tunnels and high-speed video cameras that make their wings "hum."

While the hummingbird has enhanced features unique to its physiology, such as speeds up to 30 miles an hour and non-stop migration up to five hundred miles, the Nano prototype has enough qualifications to provide the following similarities:

1. Rapid beating of their wings and a wide range of maneuverability
2. Utilizing controlled transition flight allowing for continuous hovering and flying forward, up, down and sideways.
3. Similar anatomical characteristics in wing span and body size

Where Mother Nature leaves off, aerodynamic technology picks up.

BIBLIOGRAPHY

Hennigan, William. "It's a bird! It's a spy! It's both." *Los Angeles Times*, February 17, 2001.

AeroVironment, Inc. "Nano Hummingbird." www.AVINC.com/nano, www.hitech-edge.com/Aerovironment-nano-hummingbird-fl (accessed 10/18/2011).

Pappalardo, Joe. "It's a Bird! It's a Plane! It's a Surveillance Drone Flying Inside Your Living Room." Popular Mechanics www.ponularmechanics.com/print-this/its-a-surveillance-drone (accessed 10/18/2011).

Physorg, "Robot hummingbird passes flight tests." www.physorg.com (accessed 10/18/2011).

Melanson, Donald. "DARPA-funded Nam-Hummingbird spybot takes flight."
www.engadget.com (accessed 10/18/2011).

Warrick, D.R.; Tobalske, B.W. & Powers, DR. (2005). "Aerodynamice of the hovering hummingbird." *Nature* 435; 1094-1097 doi: 10.1028/nature03647 (HTML abstract).

Chambers, Lanny. "About Hummingbirds" (www.hummingbirds.net/about.html#heartbeat). Retrieved 25 January 2009).

Skutch, Alexander F. & Singer, Arthru B. (1973): The Life of the Hummingbird. Crown Publishers, New York. ISBN 0-5l7-50572-X.

Hummingbird Facts and Information (www.howtoenjoyhummingbirds.com (accessed 10/25/2011).

High-resolution images "Courtesy of AeroVironment Inc."

Trvezove, Travis L., Photographer credited with high-resolution image of ruby-throated hummingbird, May 21, 2009.

Hummingbird Nano Air Vehicle (NAV) is a remotely controlled ultra-light aircraft developed by AeroVironment

Ruby-throated Hummingbird May 21, 2009.

About the Author

When the author rescued a kitten trapped under the tunnel of a highway, a pathway to writing followed. After completing a basic and advanced course at the Institute of Children's Literature, a series of eight articles were compiled into a book of short stories.

Gardening allows the author a little creative time, besides writing, to work with rocks and nature's surrounding patterns. The author also enjoys volunteering for the local library's shut-in services, providing delivery and pickup of books. A feeding sanctuary the author maintains in the back yard, allows for fun and treats for birds, squirrels, a few tree rats and wandering possum.

This is the author's first publication. She lives in Los Angeles with her cat Molly.